BRUCE OLIVER, TRAVEL ADVISOR & TV HOST

Turn this book into a Scratch & Sniff Book

Order your FREE Scratch & Sniff labels
And pay only for Shipping & Handling

http://ScratchAndSniffTravel.com

WHAT DO YOU SMELL?

WHEN YOU GET YOUR SCRATCH & SNIFF CARD:

1. Peel the back off of the label.
2. Push the long edge into the binder with the Scratch & Sniff Stickers facing so that you can see them.
3. Each Smelly spot will match spices listed in the book.
4. Follow directions on the label.

Enjoy and let me know what you think.
Please write a review on Amazon:
http://Amazon.com/author/bruceoliver

SENSATIONAL CRUISE LINE CUISINES

BRUCE OLIVER

SENSATIONAL CRUISE LINE CUISINES

Scratch & Sniff - Illustrated
Cook, Feast, Dream & Travel:

with tidbits, stories, wine pairings and recipes
from the Best of the Best Cruise Ships from around the world.

Be sure to check out my Travel & Food Series

A Sensational Travel & Food Resource Series™

SensationalTravelBooks.com

Traveling Coloring Books Series™
TravelingColoringBooks.com

Discover Destinations around the World

Author: Bruce Oliver, Luxury Travel Host
Illustrator: Bruce Oliver

Host of: BruceOliverTV.com – Smart TV Travel & Food Network

Author of: Sensational Travel & Food Resource Books™

and the Traveling Coloring Books™

Axis Mundi Systems LLC dba Cruise with Bruce Enterprises

Copyright © 2019 by Bruce Oliver - Travel Advisor & TV Host

Published by Vegas New Wave Media

All rights reserved. No part of this book may be reproduced in any form without permission in writing written for inclusion in a magazine, newspaper, or any other informational media. Proper credits required.

While the author has made every effort to provide accurate telephone numbers, internet addresses, and other contact information at the time of publication, neither the publisher nor the author assumes any responsibility for errors or for changes that occur after publication. The images used throughout the book are the property of the author or are licensed under a Creative Commons Attribution 4.0 International License and photographic credits are noted when available. Further, the author and publisher does not have any control over and does not assume any responsibility for third-party websites or their content.

The photograph used on the front and back covers, is courtesy of: Liv Otierk and her Amateur Travel Photography Blog located at: https://happywanderer15.wordpress.com. She said that:

"It is a picture of the spices for sale at the Grand Bazaar in Istanbul, Turkey. Again, the Bazaar is a great place to shop for tourists, but it's not super touristy. The vendors are friendly, and it's a great environment to walk around in. If you want more information look at the other post about spices"

Be sure to check out her blog for more great photos. Of course, I managed to get my face in the photo.

The recipe photo on the front cover is from the Hotel Sacher Salzburg - Fluffy Egg Soufflé listed in the book.

Printed in the United States of America.
ISBN: 1970029048
ISBN-13: 9781970029048

SENSATIONAL CRUISE LINE CUISINES

Dedicated to

My brother, Bob and my mom, Elizabeth

Travel companions and a chef.

Acknowledgments

I have many people to thank for help in producing the original book. I start with all of the hotels and institutions that contributed recipes including: Alice Boulez, Andrea Leyden, Anna Pellò, Barry Krushner, Carlotta Scarpa Olivi, Cody Thompson , Elisa Pepi, Emily Schmidt Liuzza, Gary Murphy, Jackie Collens, Jane Baldwin, Jeremy Heryet, Jessica Foss, Brittany Chavez, Jonathan Wood, Karen Candy, Laura E. Richeson, Lisa Dischinger, Melanie Wright, Meryl Press, Ms. Jerrol Golden, Nicholas Gandossi, Ondřej Kunc, Padraik McGillicuddy, Quentin Guiraud, Simone Dulies, Taylor Lee, Zuzana Šelová, Sandy Paugauguin. Their submissions help make this a valuable resource for travel, recipes and the ingredients that make them special.

I addition I'd like to thank my mom (Liz Oliver, Senior Editor in Chief) for being a sounding board. Her help caused me to make additions and changes as I went through the process to end up with what I present to you as the final product. I also thank many friends and family members that offered their advice from time to time.

Thanks to all those who helped me review content of the original book.

* Harry Schwartz.........................Celebrity Chef Harry
* Michael Cervin..........................Forbes magazine columnist
....
* Tony Pace ....Las Vegas entertainer
* Gary Murphy ....Co-Owner, AmaWaterways River Cruise Line ....
* Kelly Bergin...............................President of OASIS
....
* Rick Robinson..........................Author and Educator
* Jim and Sandy Minneo.............Entrepreneurs

Foreword

This is what my readers have said about my Scratch and Sniff Travel Series. Be sure to look for a copy on Amazon or ask for it at your local book store.

"Bruce Oliver takes us on an olfactory tour of the world, where we not only learn about the herbs and spices we all use on a daily basis but also tantalizes us with recipes and wine pairings from some of the world's best hotels and their talented chefs. Unique, intriguing and a treat for all the senses, his Scent-Sational Travels: A Scratch and Sniff Experience is a one of a kind interactive book that makes you feel like you're in the thick of all things travel and food!"
~Michael Cervin, Forbes Travel Guides

"Bruce Oliver's use of a directive of how to use this book is concise and so well laid out. I love his use of movie correlations. Brilliant Spice usage tables. This is one of the best layouts explaining where to use spices. The ethnic foods table was a surprise and my first thought I can definitely use it every day; just perfect.

The use and history of the herbs gave me a better understanding of each. I especially appreciate the history. Well done on this. The Salt section is one of my favorites. I never realized the level of differences.

I was amazed at all the recipes from an eclectic level of places from around the world. Only Bruce Oliver could have brought this together with one of the most beautiful pictorial presentations. He made me feel like I was there.

This is one of the most comprehensive and well laid out reference guides I have ever seen. Bruce Oliver has created a masterpiece of information that appeals to all our senses. This book is the standard for the food and travel industry. Simply Genius. Congratulations." **Tony Pace, Vegas Headliner and Recording Artist**

BRUCE OLIVER, TRAVEL ADVISOR & TV HOST

"Bruce Oliver cooks as well as he cruises! Being a fan of eating my way around the globe, Bruce Oliver has put together the perfect travel guide for me." **Rick Robinson, award winning author**

"In these pages, Bruce Oliver makes travel a culinary escapade. Bruce's knowledge and culinary sense makes this a guide for those hungry for travel and great food and wine." **Chef Harry Schwartz Author, Columnist, Show Host, Media Chef, Culinary Creator**

"Bruce Oliver did a nice job putting together this scratch and sniff travel and food book. What a unique idea! I love the information that is available for booking hotels and cruises. And I'll be using the recipes as well." **Kelly Bergin, President, Palm Coast Travel**

"In a word. Simply outstanding!! I have read several recipes now and I am getting so hungry. I love the scratch and sniff idea too!!!" **Jeff Froehlich, Director of Sales & Marketing, OPUS Vancouver**

"I found myself reading the book at work - caught myself and got back to work. Congratulations." **Gary Murphy, Co-Owner, AmaWaterways River Cruises**

"Bruce Oliver's Scent-Sational experience book looks fabulous." **Alice Boulez, Associate Director of Sales & Marketing, Hôtel du Louve Paris**

"What a novel idea: 'scratch and sniff travel and food'. We loved learning how executive chefs use spices, herbs and salts while they cook. The historical information, tidbits and quotes also makes the book an interesting read. It's a great resource for travelers and non-travelers alike; you can smell the ingredients before you use them. We plan to keep the book in our kitchen as a resource while cooking new and old dishes." **James and Sandy Minneo, Entrepreneurs**

Table of Illustrations

- 0-1 Illustration by Bruce Oliver 12
- 0-2 Illustration by Bruce Oliver 12
- 0-1 Photo by Bruce Oliver 15
- 0-2 Photo courtesy of AmaWaterways 17
- 0-3 Photo Courtesy of AmaWaterways 17
- 0-4 Photos courtesy AmaWaterways and Bruce Oliver 19
- 0-5 Photos courtesy of American Cruise Lines 26
- 0-6 Photo courtesy of American Cruise Lines 27
- 0-7 Photo courtesy of Crystal Cruises 32
- 0-8 Photos courtesy of Crystal Cruises 32
- 0-9 Photos by Bruce Oliver 33
- 0-10 Photos on this page by Bruce Oliver 34
- 0-11 Photos on this page by Bruce Oliver 39
- 0-12 Photo by Bruce Oliver 40
- 0-13 Photos on this page by Bruce Oliver 41
- 0-14 Photo courtesy of Holland America Lines 43
- 0-15 Photos on this page by Bruce Oliver 45
- 0-16 Photo by Bruce Oliver 54
- **0-17** Photos by Bruce Oliver 57
- **0-18** Photos courtesy of UniWorld 66

CONTENTS

Acknowledgments 5
Foreword 6
Table of Illustrations 8
How to use QR Codes 11
Interactive Version 12
Best of the Best: Cruise Ship Recipes 13
    AmaWaterways River Cruise Line Cooking Class Hungarian Goulash 15
    AmaWaterways River Cruise Line – Farmer's Cheese Fritters 18
    American Cruise Line – Jumbo Lump Crab Cakes .. 22
    American Queen Steamboat Company – American Queen Apple Pie 24
        Kick your feet up and enjoy the Mississippi River 27
    Crystal Cruise Line – Warm Lobster 29
    Crystal Cruise Line - Handmade Ravioli Filled with Ricotta 31
        A visit to see the penguins and lamas 34
        Hate to fly but you'd still like to go to Europe? 40

SENSATIONAL CRUISE LINE CUISINES

Would you love to take a cruise to the Mediterranean?............40
Holland America Line - Rib Eye Cap with Roasted Parsnip Puree............................43
Oceania Cruise Line - Spicy Duck & Watermelon Salad 47
Paul Gauguin Cruises - Polynesian Mango BBQ 51
Princess Cruise Line - Fettuccine Alfredo 53
Regent Seven Seas – Culinary Arts Kitchen – Pan Seared Scallops 59
Seabourn - Twice-Baked Goat Cheese Soufflé.................62
Uniworld River Cruise Line – Black Forest Cake..................64
Viking River Cruise - Beef Stroganoff................................68
Spice Usage Tips*.............................70
Spices used for Ethnic Foods...........75
Herbs & Spices Around the World..78
The Difference Herbs vs. Spices 78
Bibliography......................................79
Interactive Resources......................85
Index 86
Win Sweepstakes..............................88

BRUCE OLIVER, TRAVEL ADVISOR & TV HOST

How to use QR Codes

If you can use "apps" on your cell phone, iPhone, Android or Window Device and it has a camera then you can download an application to read the codes in this book. Or, you can go to the back of the book and see the Web Links for each of the hotels and cruise lines that contributed recipes for the book. Point and Scan and you get information, a website or a phone number. Once you scan the code you can visit a website, call, and/or send an email right on your phone.

For example, when you scan the tag below you will get my contact information

Share & Save my information *from the QR Code (above) to your contact list and follow me on Twitter.* **Thanks, Bruce**

Get your reader and become more productive by following the next couple of steps:
- You can download the app for your:
    - Android devices - Google Play
    - Apple devices – AppStore
    - Windows devices – Windows Apps
- Use one or more of the following search terms:
    - QR code scanner
    - Code scanner
    - QR and barcode scanner
- Install one of the readers NOTE: some bar code scanners don't read QR Codes.

SENSATIONAL CRUISE LINE CUISINES

Interactive Version

This book is available online, Kindle, NOOK, iPad, Smartphones, and in print. The interactive version has video, audio and additional information about the recipes, techniques, ideas trivia and other fun things to add to the experience. You can get this information on the computer, the internet, iPad, Android device, Blackberry and your smart devices.

The customer can also register for additional services. Product discounts and other value-added promotions. Pages with this iPad image or the BruceOliverTV logo indicates there is additional information online. The fee to access the channel full with video information and more can be accessed for a nominal monthly fee.

0-1 Illustration by Bruce Oliver

http://SmartTVtraveler.com

http://Promotions.CruiseWithBruce.com

0-2 Illustration by Bruce Oliver

BRUCE OLIVER, TRAVEL ADVISOR & TV HOST

Best of the Best: Cruise Ship Recipes

SENSATIONAL CRUISE LINE CUISINES

BRUCE OLIVER, TRAVEL ADVISOR & TV HOST

AmaWaterways [i] River Cruise Line Cooking Class Hungarian Goulash
AmaWaterways Christmas Markets Cruise
Cooking Class at the Sofitel Budapest Chain Bridge
<u>PARIS BUDAPEST RESTAURANT</u>

Ingredients:
300 g or 0.66 pounds, shank of beef
500 g or 1.1 pounds peeled potatoes
30 g lard or 4 to 5 teaspoons other cooking fat or vegetable oil
One large onion, finely chopped
One or two tomatoes
1/2 teaspoon powdered sweet paprika
Salt to taste
1/2 teaspoon caraway seeds
One medium carrot, cut into quarters
One medium parsnip or celery root, cut into quarters

0-1 Photo by Bruce Oliver

One cloves garlic 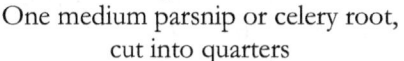, crushed

Preparation:
1. Cube the meat (only for traditional goulash) and potatoes into 2 cm (3/4 inch) pieces.
2. Stew the onion in lard over low heat until golden yellow (not brown).
3. Add the chopped sweet paprika and tomato and fine chopped garlic.
4. Remove the pot from the heat, add the meat, salt, caraway

> **Wine Recommendation**: Dry Creek Valley (California) Zinfandel 2006 from (Artezin Wines, 2016) Showing a classic Dry Creek profile, this Zinfandel offers bright berry fruit enhanced by briary spice. That combination worked especially well with our goulash, as the fruit enhanced the stew's sweetness while the spicy notes added an element of intrigue. Adding to its appeal, the wine is very well-balanced, so not at all hot or heavy.

seeds, and add water until it is covered.
5. If the meat is 80% tender, switch it off and let it rest. Sprinkle with paprika.
6. Return to low heat and simmer.
7. After 30 minutes, add the vegetables.
8. When the meat is nearly tender (around another 30 minutes), add the potatoes.
9. Taste it, and if you need you can add more spices.
10. When every ingredient is tender, you're ready! You can serve the **Hungarian Goulash Soup** immediately, or reheat later.

Cruise with Bruce Trivia
Goulash or Gulyás means "Herdsman" in Hungarian and because the dish was (still is) a very popular Hungarian Herdsman's meal. The meal is prepared in a cast-iron pot over an open fire, out in the field, without much fuss. Goulash can be prepared from beef, veal, pork, or lamb.
Paprika is a spice made from air-dried fruits of the chili pepper family of the species *Capsicum annuum*. It is often associated with Hungarian cuisine. The seasoning is also used to add color and flavor to many types of dishes. It is a featured spice in the Budapest Market.
Celery Root AKA celeriac tastes like a cross between a strong celery and parsley. (Foodterms, 2016)

0-2 Photo courtesy of AmaWaterways

Captain's Welcome

0-3 Photo Courtesy of AmaWaterways

Twin Balcony

SENSATIONAL CRUISE LINE CUISINES

FARMER'S CHEESE FRITTERS "SYRNIKI"

AmaWaterways River Cruise Line – Farmer's Cheese Fritters "Syunik"

Ingredients (makes four servings):
1 cup 100 g all Farmers Cheese
1 teaspoon of sour cream
One egg
1 tablespoon of sugar
2 tablespoons of flour
Salt to taste
Clarified butter for frying

Wine Recommendation: From the (Premier Cru Vineyard, n.d.), Billaud Simon – a Chablis Premier Cru Chablis Montee de Tonnerre, This Chablis is lean, minerally, and lovely with Farmers Cheese. This style of Chardonnay from cool eastern France has overt green apple flavors

Preparation:
1. Beat egg with sugar until creamy, using a food processor will work best.
2. Add farmer's cheese, sour cream, flour, salt and process until smooth.
3. Form balls about 2 inches or 5 cm in diameter, flattening them out and fry in butter until both sides are golden.
4. Serve the half readers with sour cream and jam.

AmaWaterways Award Winning Ships and Food.

Limited Edition Tours
These included excursions provide unique opportunities to immerse yourself in the destination and are offered in addition to standard city tours. Examples include learning how to make goulash in Budapest or going to a bratwurst and beer tasting.

0-4 Photos courtesy AmaWaterways and Bruce Oliver

SENSATIONAL CRUISE LINE CUISINES

Amawaterways' Executive Chef on board the AmaVida

AmaWaterways is a member of La Chaine des Rotisseurs, one of the world's most prestigious culinary organizations. *Membership is by invitation only, extended only to those possessing world-class culinary acumen. All their ships in Europe are members of the Chaine des Rotisseurs, and their culinary staff is united by a desire to share their expert knowledge of wine and fine dining with you.*

The Chef's Table
This specialty restaurant serves as an intimate dining alternative to the Main Restaurant. It seats a limited number of people and features a view of the chef as he prepares an array of delicious dishes for your gastronomic pleasure. Dining at this restaurant is <u>included</u> in the cruise fare.

BRUCE OLIVER, TRAVEL ADVISOR & TV HOST

SENSATIONAL CRUISE LINE CUISINES

American Cruise Line – Jumbo Lump Crab Cakes [ii]

Ingredients (serves six people):

1 pound of crab meat, jumbo lump
Two cups Ritz crackers, crushed
¼ cup green onions, finely chopped
½ cup whole bell pepper, red, finely chopped
1/3 cup mayonnaise
One egg
1 teaspoon Worcestershire sauce
1 teaspoon dry mustard
One tsp old bay seasoning
¼ lemon, juiced up
½ teaspoon garlic powder
1 teaspoon salt
½ cup teaspoon cayenne pepper
½ cup flour, for dusting oil for frying pan

Preparation:

1. In a large bowl, mix together all the ingredients except for the flour.
2. Shape into 1 ½ ounce paddies and dust with flour.
3. Heat the oil in a large skillet over medium heat.
4. When the oil is hot, carefully placed the crab cakes, in batches, in the pan and fry until brown, about 4 to 5 minutes.
5. Carefully flip the crab cakes and fry on the other side until golden brown, about 4 minutes.
6. Serve warm with remoulade sauce.
1. To serve: Dress the field greens lightly with the lemon vinaigrette just prior to serve. Serve on a plate with remoulade sauce and field greens.

> **Wine Recommendation**: From (Willamette Valley Vineyards, 2016) a Sweet Riesling Wine. This semi-sweet wine opens with prominent aromas of citrus, peach and honeysuckle. The mouthfeel is juicy with bright acidity that activates the palate and displays flavors of pineapple and pear. The finish is wonderfully persistent with balance of sweetness and refreshing crispness.

BRUCE OLIVER, TRAVEL ADVISOR & TV HOST

AMERICAN QUEEN™ STEAMBOAT COMPANY

SENSATIONAL CRUISE LINE CUISINES

American Queen Steamboat Company – American Queen Apple Pie [iii]

Crust for one 9-10inch deep dish double crusted pie:

2.5 cups all-purpose flour
13 tablespoons unsalted butter (very cold)
8 tablespoons vegetable shortening (very cold)
2 tablespoons granulated sugar
1 teaspoon kosher salt
3 tablespoons water
3 tablespoons vodka

Preparation:

1. Combine water and vodka and add ice, reserve. In the bowl of a food processor combine the flour, sugar, and salt. Drop the shortening in in tablespoon sized pieces and cut the butter into small cubes and add to the bowl. Pulse 6-8 times or until the dough resembles coarse meal or fine granola (it is great if you still see very small pieces of the butter). Empty the dough out into a large bowl and then sprinkle 5-6 tablespoons of the chilled water-vodka over the top. With a spatula fold the dough together until it forms a cohesive mass. Split this in two equal sized portions and form it with your hands into two discs. Wrap tightly with plastic and refrigerate for a couple of hours or overnight.

2. Lightly flour the surface of a cutting board, the top of the dough disc, and the rolling pin. Roll the disc out to a 11-12-inch circle and transfer to a chilled pie plate. Fill with fruit filling and repeat with the top. Cut 4-5 small slits in the top and crimp the crust to form a tight seal. You may brush the surface with some cream and sprinkle with sugar but it is not necessary. Bake for 50 -60 minutes at 350 degrees or until the pie crust is golden brown and the filling is hot and bubbling a bit. I recommend putting the pie on a sheet pan to catch the filling that may bubble out to save the cleanup of your oven. If the crust browns before the filling bubbles cover it with a sheet of aluminum foil and continue to bake.

For the filling:
½ a stick of unsalted butter
1.5lbs of peeled and sliced Granny Smith apples
1.5lb of peeled and sliced Honey Crisp Apples
½ cup of sugar
1 teaspoon of cinnamon
1/8 teaspoon of grated nutmeg
1/8 teaspoon of ground clove
Zest from ½ a lemon
Juice from ½ a lemon
¼ cup of all-purpose flour

Preparation:
1. Peel, core and slice the apples. Reserve them in a large bowl, you should have 3lbs.
2. Heat a large Dutch oven over medium low heat.
3. Melt the butter and add the sugar, lemon zest and juice, cinnamon, nutmeg and clove.
4. Stir together and cook for about 2-3 minutes.
5. Add the apples all at once and mix well.
6. Cover and cook stirring every two to three minutes until they begin to shrink and give off some juice, about 10-12 minutes.
7. Taste for sugar, spices and lemon and adjust if needed.
8. Sprinkle the flour over the top and mix well.
9. At this point it is ready to fill the pie or it may be refrigerated for a day. Bring to room temp before use.
10. This should be enough filling to create a slightly mounded pie.
11. It will shrink a bit more while cooking, but there will be a nice layer of fruit.

> **Wine Recommendation:** (Chateau Ste Michelle (Woodinville, WA), 2016), Gewürztraminer. The aromas of lychee and rose water pop. The palate brings a slight spritz, with lighter-bodied flavors that linger on the finish. The style is reserved but it shows a good sense of balance. 87 Points Wine Enthusiast

SENSATIONAL CRUISE LINE CUISINES

American Queen Chef Paul + New 'Blaser' Painting

0-5 Photos courtesy of American Cruise Lines

American Queen Dining Room

While you cruise the river enjoy a snack and watch the scenery.

Kick your feet up and enjoy the Mississippi River on the American Queen.

I know that many people want to travel in the United States and drive or fly to the destination then go on a tour or see the destination on their own. But river cruising is a more relaxed way of visiting the major cities. Try kicking your feet up as you float up or down the major rivers in the United States and unpack just once.

When America was being settled, cities sprung up on the rivers because commerce could take place via the rivers from region to region.

I love river cruising in the U.S. and around the world because it allows me to connect with new friends over a meal or a glass of wine during the time that I might be on a bus traveling for several hours.

0-6 Photo courtesy of American Cruise Lines

SENSATIONAL CRUISE LINE CUISINES

BRUCE OLIVER, TRAVEL ADVISOR & TV HOST

Crystal Cruise Line – Warm Lobster[iv] poached in Sage Butter
On Bean, Zucchini and Tomato Salad

Ingredients:

For the lobster (12 pax)
1/2 each cold water lobster (Clear Water)
2 cups butter, salted
1 cup extra virgin olive oil
1 bunch herb, sage, fresh

Bean, Tomato and Zucchini Salad:
3/4 cup black eyed beans, soaked overnight, cook soft with bay leaf
to marinate extra virgin olive oil
to marinate white balsamic vinegrette
1 Tbs onion, brunoise sauté

Separate marinate Vegetables:
1/4 each tomato, peeled, seeded stripes
1/4 each julienne zucchini green long julienne
1/4 each julienne zucchini yellow long julienne
to marinate extra virgin olive oil
to marinate white balsamic vinaigrette
1 tsp Italian flat leaf parsley roughly chopped
to taste salt
to taste pepper, white freshly ground
to drizzle extra virgin olive oil
to top small lettuce and micro greens

Procedure:
1. Soak beans (black eyed) overnight.
2. Cook with bay leaf and cool down in stock (no salt), store in stock until use, rinse before use.
3. Drain, marinate with evoo, white balsamic vinaigrette, salt and freshly cracked pepper and leave at room temperature to marinate.
4. Marinate separate tomato and green & yellow zucchini.
5. Poach lobster in sage butter and keep warm above small salamander.
6. Place first bean salad, followed by marinated vegetable salad and than poached lobster.
7. Drizzle with sage butter.
8. Garnish with tossed small lettuce and micro greens.
9. Drizzle to with extra virgin olive oil.

Wine Recommendation: (Henry of Pelham Estate Winery, ON Canada, 2016), Cuvée Catharine 2010 Estate Blanc de Blanc 'Carte Blanche' Chardonnay.

"A very sophisticated Champagne style vintage Blanc de Blanc from Henry of Pelham with considerable class and refinement. Rich, heady with evidence of significant time on the lees and nicely integrated flavors and acids. Impressive progression of flavors on the palate with exceptional length. Notes of fresh buttered bread, white flower, lemon custard and green apple" – 90 Points – Sara D'Amato – WineAlign.com

Crystal Cruise Line - Handmade Ravioli Filled with Ricotta
On Pumpkin Puree, Drizzled with Pumpkin Seed Pesto

Ingredients:

For the Ricotta Filling (30 each ravioli):

10 cup each cheese, ricotta, Prego
4 cup   cheese, Mascarpone
6 cup   Cheese, parmesan, grated
to taste salt
to taste pepper, white, freshly ground
to taste nutmeg, freshly ground

For the Pumpkin Seed Pesto (1 liter):

1 cup pumpkin seed, peeled, toasted
1.5 cup each pumpkin seed oil, only from Austria
1 lbs basil, fresh
1 cup each parmesan, grated
to taste salt
to taste pepper, white, freshly ground
to taste sugar, granulated

For the Pumpkin Puree (1.45 liter):

1 liter butternut squash puree, strained (oven roast with olive oil and fresh thyme)
1/4 liter QimiQ
1/4 cup maple syrup, (real maple)
1/2 cup lemon oil
1/8 cup orange concentrate (Vitality)
2 pinch nutmeg, freshly ground
2 pinch cinnamon, powder
to taste salt
to taste pepper, white, freshly ground

Wine Recommendation: (Masciarelli Winery, 2016), Trebbiano d'Abruzzo "Marina Cvetic". the wine was dry, warm, smooth; freshly acidic and tasty. It was full-bodied and balanced, with intense and fine mouth flavors of clementine, peach, butter, roasted hazelnut and plenty of minerality which was reminiscent of salt water. Those enticing flavors lingered in the mouth with delightful persistence.

Preparation:
1. Spoon puree on the bottom of a deep plate

SENSATIONAL CRUISE LINE CUISINES

2. Cook ravioli al dente
3. Sauté in brown sage butter
4. Place on top of puree
5. Drizzle with pumpkin seed pesto

0-8 Photos courtesy of Crystal Cruises
Crystal Serenity Trident Chef

0-7 Photo courtesy of Crystal Cruises
Crystal Symphony Nobu Arms Chef

Visiting South America – Antarctica – the Falkland Islands

I was lucky enough to be able to cruise on the Crystal Symphony to Antarctica from Buenos Aries, Argentina with my mom, my cousin Carol and a friend Ann.

Prego Specialty Dining Room

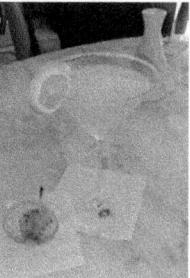

0-9 Photos by Bruce Oliver

The service is impeccable; the food is great and it's all inclusive. What a way to travel. I was spoiled. And so were my guests. Every afternoon we went to the Palm Court pictured above to see the 180° view of where we were going.

SENSATIONAL CRUISE LINE CUISINES

A great way to visit the waters of Antarctica and the Drake Passage. Below I am at the southern tip of South America in Ushuaia, on the lake at the end of the Tierra del Fuego below.

0-10 Photos on this page by Bruce Oliver

A visit to see the penguins and lamas

Notes:

SENSATIONAL CRUISE LINE CUISINES

Cunard Cruise Line - Seared Scallops Celeriac and Truffle Puree

ᵛ soy and honey dressing, grain mustard vinaigrette

Ingredients:	Measure Factor	Unit	Basic Prep
Scallops			
Scallops-Shelled-Roe-off-10-20 lbs.	1	Kg	
Butter, unsalted	50	Gram	
Oil Cooking/Frying	100	Milliliter	
Salt, cooking fine	10	Gram	
White Ground Pepper	2	Gram	
Celeriac and Truffle Puree			
Celery Root (Celeriac	200	Gram	
Milk Whole UHT	400	Milliliter	
Butter, unsalted	30	Gram	
Truffle Black Summar Whole Brushed Guillot E	5	Gram	Chop
Oil Truffle White	0.02	Each	5 ml
Salt, cooking fine	10	Gram	
White Ground Pepper	2	Gram	
Honey and Soy Dressing			
Honey, clear	80	Gram	
Olive Oil	80	Milliliter	
Ground Five Spice	4	Gram	
Dijon Mustard	25	Gram	
Soya Sauce, light	4	Milliliter	
White Ground Pepper	2	Gram	
Agar	8	Gram	
Garnish			
Celery Root (Celeriac)	500	Gram	Deep Fry Crisp – 3 per portion

Seared Scallops' Preparation:
Scallops:
1. Season the scallops and pan-fry in butter and oil.

Celeriac and Truffle Puree:
1. Add the celeriac to the milk and cook until soft.
2. Drain off the milk and reserve for blending and place the celeriac in a blender.
3. Blend until smooth then add the hard butter. You might need to add the liquid for a softer smoother texture.
4. Add the truffle juice, oil and chopped black truffle to the celeriac puree and season.

Honey and Soy Dressing:
1. In a bowl, whisk in the vinegars, mustard, soy sauce, honey and spice.
2. Slice the celeriac on the slicing machine 5mm thick and cut out using the 50mm cutter. Deep fry at 140° until soft then remove and leave to drain on kitchen paper.

Garnish as shown in the image.

> **Wine Recommendation**: (Clinton Vineyards, 2016), Seyval Blanc. The Victory White Estate-Bottled 2014 vintage is well-balanced, showcasing delicate tropical fruit aromas that carry over to the palate. It has a delightful bright, lively acidity, a clean finish and an elegant mouthfeel. Seyval Blanc 2014 — Victory White is ideal as an aperitif, or as the perfect companion for seafood, poultry, salads and spicy dishes.

Anniversary Party

Dessert and some wine.

Dinner in Britannia Dining Room

0-11 Photos on this page by Bruce Oliver

Culinary Art Demonstration

Sensational Cruise Line Cuisines

Hate to fly but you'd still like to go to Europe?
Try taking a Cunard Transatlantic Cruise on the Queen Mary 2!

My first crossing in January 2014 was as the guest of Stanley Birge, North American Vice President of the Cunard Cruise Line. That was the 10th Anniversary sailing of the world's only ocean liner, Cunard's Queen Mary 2.

In June of 2016, the remastered ship left Hamburg following a 25-day dry dock refurbishment with new paint, 55,200 square meters of newly laid carpet, etc. The ship was "remastered" with new single cabins, 30 Britannia Club Balcony cabins added, the Grill restaurants have been transformed, Kings Court Buffet has been completely redesigned; the Todd English restaurant has been replaced with The Verandah and the Winter Garden with the Carinthia Lounge.

Would you love to take a cruise to the Mediterranean?
I had the pleasure of sailing for 18 days aboard Cunard's smaller ship, the Queen Victoria. Take the Transatlantic NYC to Southampton then board QV for your cruise to the Med.

0-12 Photo by Bruce Oliver

Here I am with Stanley Birge at the reception the first night on the QM2 in NYC.

0-13 *Photos on this page by Bruce Oliver*

Point Europa behind the Rock of Gibraltar

While you're at it visit my favorite mansion outside of London. At the Cliveden House you'll be treated like Royalty. (Radio Show, 2014)

Barcelona was crazy, I even saw a man going around like this!

SENSATIONAL CRUISE LINE CUISINES

Holland America Line - Rib Eye Cap with Roasted Parsnip Puree [vi]

Shelf Life: Yield: Yield: Serves 10
Ingredients:

Rib eye cap 1400 grams
Sea salt 10 grams
Pepper black Crushed 10 grams
Olive oil 50 ml
Rosemary Twig 1 each
Parsnip Peeled, cut in half lengthwise. 1000 grams
Sea salt 8 grams
Pepper white 5 grams
Heavy cream 600 ml
Butter 50 grams
Olive oil 30 ml
Cayenne pepper 3 grams
Heritage baby carrots Roasted whole 200 grams
Chipolini onions Peeled, whole 10 each
Olive oil 600 ml
Thyme fresh Twig 1 each
Pepper corn black 5 grams
Garlic Peeled, whole 1 each
Beef jus 500 ml
Truffle juice Readymade 80 ml
Red wine 200 ml
Black truffle Sliced 20 grams
Butter unsalted 100 grams
Romanesco Florets, blanched 5 second only 200 grams
Sweet and sour pickling juice 500 ml
Pea tendrils 50 grams

From John Mulvaney, Corporate Executive Chef - "This particular dish used the pea tendrils to accompany the beef. This was perfect match in flavors, with the sweetness of the pea tendrils and umami flavor of the beef. Perfect match, but this unique beef cut, is the cap from the Prime rib beef. Using only the cap from the prime rib of beef insures you have the tastiest cut of beef from the cow and with the tenderness of the tenderloin."

0-14 Photo courtesy of Holland America Lines

For Service:
1. Season beef cap with salt, pepper, rub with olive oil.
2. Charcoal grill the cap, place on grill, once nicely marked, turn around, grill to medium rare, set on the side to rest for 10/15, place rosemary on top to add some flavor, prior service flash quickly on the grill for temperature, then slice as needed (could be also seared on hot plate or grill, marked from 2 side, placed in rational oven by low temperature of 80 C, roasted to internal temperature of 52 C, place rosemary on top, set on side to rest for few minutes)
3. Place parsnip on baking tray, sprinkle with salt, olive oil and place in oven by 180C for 15 minutes, then remove from tray, place in thermos mix together with all other ingredients and cook by 53 C for 60 minutes then blend to fine puree, strain if necessary, season with salt and cayenne
4. Cippolini onion place in food pan with all other ingredients except oil. Heat oil to 70 C poor over onion, ensure onion is covered completely, place food pan in oven by 80 C for about 30 minutes till onions are tender cooked, remove from oil.
5. Heat roasted carrots as needed
6. Romanesco blanch, cook in blast chiller and place in cold pickling sweet and sour juice, need to be at room temperature for serving
7. Reduce red wine by half, add beef jus, truffle juice and keep reducing again to half, when sauce needed prior service mount with fresh butter cubes and add truffle last minute.
8. Plate as shown in picture and garnish with pea tendrils.

> **Wine Recommendation**: Loren Sonkin, Founder/Winemaker at Sonkin Cellars recommends (Beringer, 2016), Beringer Knight's Valley Cabernet Sauvignon. She says the best wine to pair with a ribeye steak is one that has a high percentage of Cabernet Sauvignon. Whether it is from Napa or Bordeaux (or elsewhere) the tannins in the wine help cut thru the fat and juices of the steak to make a great combination.

In 1960 the Holland America Line was the the first cruise line to offer sailings to Alaska. Princess Cruise Line started to offer cruises to Alaska in 1969. Holland America's smaller ships have preferred positions on the docks of Alaska's ports of call. Learn more about Holland America Line by listening to my radio program (Holland America Line Interview, 2011)

In September, 2016 I took my second trip to Alaska and will feature this amazing destination in another "scratch and sniff" travel and food book.

Skagway Alaska White Pass & Yukon Train

Skagway and the Famous Red Onion Saloon

0-15 Photos on this page by Bruce Oliver

Salmon Bake in Juneau *Ketchikan Port*

SENSATIONAL CRUISE LINE CUISINES

Oceania Cruise Line - Spicy Duck & Watermelon Salad [vii]

This salad has become one of the true favorites of Red Ginger. Duck confit is a traditional ingredient in French cassoulet, but we pair it here with watermelon for a fresh and savory salad that is a true crowd pleaser. The crisp texture and sweetness of watermelon perfectly balance the chewy richness of duck confit.

Sweet Fish Sauce Ingredients (serves 6):

¾ cup palm sugar, coarsely chopped
¼ cup water
½ large shallot, coarsely chopped
1 lemongrass stalk, bulb portion only, coarsely chopped
1 kaffir lime leaf
½-inch piece galangal, peeled and coarsely chopped
1 to 2 tablespoons fish sauce
1 to 2 tablespoons tamarind concentrate

Duck and Watermelon Salad Ingredients:

Canola oil, for frying
½ cup raw cashew nuts
Kosher salt
6 confit duck legs
2 to 4 tablespoons hoisin sauce
6 cups 1-inch-cube seedless watermelon
½ cup Thai basil or sweet basil leaves
½ cup mint leaves
½ cup cilantro leaves
1/3 cup thinly sliced shallot

For the Sauce:
1. In a medium saucepan, combine the palm sugar and water, place over medium heat, and heat, stirring occasionally, until the sugar is melted – about 5 minutes.
2. Remove from the heat. Stir in the shallot, lemongrass, lime leaf and galangal and let sit at room temperature to cool and to infuse the flavors for at least 1 hour, or preferably overnight.
3. Strain the liquid through a fine-mesh strainer into a small bowl. Discard the solids. Add 1 tablespoon each of the fish sauce and tamarind, mixing well. Taste and adjust seasoning with additional fish sauce and tamarind if needed. Set the sauce aside at room temperature.

For the Salad:

SENSATIONAL CRUISE LINE CUISINES

1. Pour 4 inches of canola oil into a large, deep saucepan and heat to 325°F on a deep-frying thermometer.
2. Line a small plate with paper towels for draining the cashews and line a larger plate for draining the duck.
3. Add the cashews to the hot oil and fry until crisp, about 1 minute.
4. Using a slotted spoon, transfer to the towel-lined plate.
5. Sprinkle with salt while hot.
6. Increase the temperature of the oil to 350°F.
7. Add 2 duck legs to the hot oil and fry, turning to brown on all sides, until crisp, 4 to 5 minutes.
8. Using tongs, transfer to the towel-lined plate to drain.
9. Repeat with the remaining duck legs in two batches.

When the duck legs are cool enough to handle, peel off the skin from each leg in as large a piece as possible.

10. Cut the skin into strips and set aside.
11. Bone the legs and shred the meat into a bowl.
12. Season to taste with the hoisin sauce.

13. In a separate bowl, combine the watermelon, basil, mint, and cilantro.
14. Add the duck meat, duck skin, cashews, and shallot.
15. Toss with enough of the sweet fish sauce to coat lightly.
16. You may not need all the sauce.

> **Wine Recommendation**: (Sharpe Hill Vineyard (Pomfret, CT), 2016), Riesling. These wines should be served chilled and are often paired with fresh berries, plum tarts, and strawberry shortcake. Bracetto d'Acqui is one of the few wines that works extremely well with chocolate and it is a classic pairing with gianduia, the popular sweet chocolate with hazelnut paste, produced in the nearby city of Turin.

To Serve: Divide the salad among individual serving plates or martini glasses.

Top Five Reasons Guests Choose Oceania Cruises
1. **The Finest Cuisine at Sea™.** Each dish begins with premium artisanal ingredients from around the world and ends with an artful à la minute presentation, so you're certain to savor your dining experiences long after your voyage. Plus, all of our gourmet specialty restaurants are complimentary.
2. **Our renowned epicurean enrichment programs.** – From our highly popular Culinary Discovery Tours™ and hands-on cooking classes at The Culinary Center on board Marina and Riviera to our multi-day immersive Culinary Creations Land Tours, our voyages provide endless opportunities to delve into the local culture through the lens of cuisine.
3. **Boutique ports and unique itineraries.** – Our intimate and luxurious ships sail to over 365 alluring destinations, exploring off-the-beaten-path destinations that larger ships simply cannot access, bringing you authentic and unforgettable experiences.
4. **Exceptional personalized attention.** – Our staff-to-guest ratio is extraordinarily high, with staff chosen from the world's finest hotels and renowned restaurants. The members of our staff genuinely care about making you happy, and you'll feel like family from the day you embark.
5. **The intimate and luxurious ambiance.** – Our guests delight in the sumptuous, yet comfortable atmosphere of each of our ships. The stylish furnishings, convivial mood and lavish extras make you feel as though you are at your own private country club.

SENSATIONAL CRUISE LINE CUISINES

Paul Gauguin Cruises

Paul Gauguin Cruises - Polynesian Mango BBQ Sauce [viii]

Ingredients:

- 4 large onions chopped
- 1 head garlic chopped
- 1 bunch ginger chopped
- 4 each bay leaves
- 5 each star anise
- 1 lbs. brown sugar
- 5 each ripe mango
- 3 cup mango puree
- 1 cup mustard (Guldens)
- 1 cup ketchup
- ½ bottle rum
- 1-gallon barbecue sauce (Your favorite brand)

> **Wine Recommendation**: (Billsboro Winery (Geneva, NY), 2016), Pinot Gris. This 100% Pinot Gris bursts across the palate with mouthwatering melon and juicy peach. Summer ripened strawberry punctuates the finish of this Billsboro favorite. Pair with fish tacos and mango salsa.

Procedure:
1. In a sauce pot over medium heat sauté onion, garlic and ginger until translucent.
1. Add the bay leaves, star anise and brown sugar.
2. Cook until brown sugar is dissolved.
3. Deglaze pan with rum.
4. Bring to a simmer and cook until rum is reduced by half.
5. Then add the ripe mango, mango puree, ketchup, mustard, barbecue sauce and bring back to a simmer.
6. Once simmering, allow to cook until mixture is reduced by half
7. Remove the bay leaves and star anise.
8. Puree until smooth refrigerate and use as needed.
9. When grilling, use a light glaze over the top of your meats, fish or vegetables before turning.

SENSATIONAL CRUISE LINE CUISINES

Princess Cruise Line - Fettuccine Alfredo [ix]

Ingredients (Serves 4):

1 lb. Egg noodles
4 ea. Egg yolks
1 cup Heavy cream
½ cup Parmesan cheese, grated
Salt and pepper to taste

Parmesan Cheese Baskets

2 cups parmesan cheese, grated

Preparation:

Fettuccine Alfredo
1. Cook the pasta per package directions.
2. Drain and set aside.
3. Boil ¾ cup of the cream and remove from heat. Combine egg yolks with remaining ¼ cup cream to form a liaison.
4. Add ¼ cup of the boiled cream to the liaison. Stir and then combine liaison with the rest of the cream. Add parmesan cheese, adjust seasoning.
5. If necessary reheat pasta in boiling, salted water. Pour sauce over drained pasta.

Parmesan Cheese Basket
1. Place a non-stick omelet pan on the stove top over medium heat. Sprinkle the bottom of the pan evenly
2. with approximately ½ cup of the parmesan cheese. Cook until the color changes too golden.
3. Flip the cheese over and cook until golden. Remove the cheese from the pan and place over a mold form or over the bottom of a bowl to create a dome shape. Let cool.

> **Wine Recommendation:** (Mount Palomar Vineyard, 2016), Castelletto Cortese. This Cortese is clean and well balanced, with firm structure, citrus nuances and the refreshing mineral quality of deep well-water. Its name means "courteous" in Italian and it does have a soft, gentle quality when the grapes are allowed to ripen fully. It is a wonderful match with seafood pastas, such as Linguine alle Vongole, Fettuccine Alfredo with shrimp and almost any grilled fish. It also matches well with Lemon and Rosemary Chicken and Baked Brie with Honey Glaze.

SENSATIONAL CRUISE LINE CUISINES

The Princess Cruise's Dining Experience - Chef's Table:
- See the galley operations in action, while enjoying hors d'oeuvres and champagne with the chef himself.
- Participants will also be served an exclusive menu created by the chef using special ingredients from local markets, and paired with wine.
- To participate in the Chef's Table, be sure to call the Front Desk or Maitre d' as soon as you board the ship.
- Space is usually limited to 8 passengers per cruise. There is an extra charge for this service.

0-16 Photo by Bruce Oliver

Appetizers and wine pairings before sitting down at the Chef's Table with Antonio.

Executive Chef Antonio Cereda & Maitre D'Hotel Jose De Amaral are with us in this photo on the Caribbean Princess Cruise Ship

SENSATIONAL CRUISE LINE CUISINES

Princess Cruise Line goes all over the world from the Caribbean to Alaska and the British Isles. Cruise lengths can be as little as 3 days on the Pacific Coast of the United States all the way up to over 100 days on World Cruises and World Cruise Segments. I'll be writing about taking a Princess Cruise to Alaska in another book when you'll take another smell-journey.

The photograph on the left was taken of me in front of the "Standing Stones of Stennis" on the Orkney Isles just north of Scotland. The fresh smelling sea air and quietness added to the intrigue of the site.

Did you know that England and the United States' air bases were located on the Orkney Islands during World War II? ... Neither did I!

The cruise started off in Southampton and went all over the British Isles including the Channel Isles Ireland, Northern Ireland, Wales, Scotland, the Orkney Isles and England. An interesting way to smell the Blarney Stone and seafood offered in that destination.

Besides Alaska the Caribbean is a favorite destination for Princess.

0-17 Photos by Bruce Oliver

You may want to visit St. Maarten on one of your cruises.

Watch my interview of the Staff of the Caribbean Princess Ship on my *(Cruise with Bruce YouTube Channel, 2014)*

SENSATIONAL CRUISE LINE CUISINES

Regent
SEVEN SEAS CRUISES®

BRUCE OLIVER, TRAVEL ADVISOR & TV HOST

Regent Seven Seas – Culinary Arts Kitchen – Pan Seared Scallops with Red Curry Glaze [x]

Ingredients (serves 2):

FOR RED CURRY GLAZE:

¼ cup fresh pineapple juice
¼ cup cream of coconut
1 tablespoon red curry paste
1 tablespoon white miso

In a small saucepan, whisk together and heat all ingredients over low heat. Hold until needed.

FOR SCALLOPS:

4 large 'dry' diver sea scallops (see Chef Tip)
1 scant tablespoon clarified butter
1 tablespoon toasted coconut flakes
1 tablespoon basil and cilantro micro greens
chili oil

> **Wine Recommendation:** (LaBelle Winery (Amherst, NH), 2016), LaBelle Riesling. This Riesling is a semi-sweet, aromatic white wine with apple, peach & pear notes as you first raise the glass. On your palate, this wine is complex – adding floral and honey overtones – alongside citrus nuances and a delicate minerality. That's why this wine is great with a variety of food pairings ranging from appetizers to desserts. It is so flexible that it compliments most meals – a nice easy choice! Especially great with poultry or seafood. Because of Riesling's sweetness and acidity, it makes the perfect accompaniment to spicy food. Strong Indian and Asian spices are a perfect match with Riesling. A classic pairing with Riesling is spiced duck leg.

CULINARY ARTS KITCHEN
— onboard —
REGENT SEVEN SEAS CRUISES®

Preparation:
1. An hour before searing, remove the scallops from refrigeration and pat dry.
2. Allow the scallops to come to room temperature on a paper towel.
3. Check to be sure the scallops are dry when they come to room temperature.
4. In a small sauté pan, heat the clarified butter until the fat and pan are searing hot.

5. Only a small amount of butter is needed, so if there is more butter than coats the pan pour it off.
6. Using tongs, carefully place the dry, room temperature scallops in the searing hot pan.
7. Allow the scallops to develop a caramel color but not disrupting the searing process (do not stir).
8. When one side of the scallop is cooked, carefully turn the scallops to sear on the other side.
9. Remove the scallops, place on top of red curry glaze and garnish with coconut and serve immediately.
10. If using the Golden Semolina Cakes (see recipe), place scallop on top of cake, drizzle glaze and garnish with coconut and micro greens.
11. Add a dot of chili oil, if desired.

BRUCE OLIVER, TRAVEL ADVISOR & TV HOST

SENSATIONAL CRUISE LINE CUISINES

Seabourn - Twice-Baked Goat Cheese Soufflé[xi]

Ingredients (serves 6):
- ½ ounce butter
- ½ ounce all high gluten flour
- 2 garlic cloves, minced
- 3-ounce goat cheese
- 2 egg whites
- 1 ½ egg yolks
- 2 ½ ounce whole milk
- ½ ounce grated parmesan cheese
- 1 ounce grated gruyere cheese
- ½ cup sour cream
- nutmeg

> "Our famous Seabourn Goat Cheese Soufflé is clearly a guest favorite on board our ships. And one of the most requested recipes." - Bjoern Wassmuth, Manager of Culinary Operations We're pleased to share the recipe for this delicious dish. Enjoy!

Preparation:
1. Warm the milk with the garlic and a little nutmeg.
2. Mix the butter with the flour separately, fold with the milk to a sticky mass and cook for 5 minutes, stirring constantly to avoid lump formation.
3. Blend in the cheese.
4. Remove from the heat and blend with the egg yolks.
5. Season to taste.
6. Whisk the egg whites with a little salt in a mixing bowl to help it stiffen.
7. Slowly fold in the egg whites to the cheese mass.
8. In the meantime, prepare the mold (can use a flexi-rubber mold), which has been brushed with butter and dusted with flour and grated parmesan cheese.
9. Fill into molds. Place in water-filled baking sheet. Bake first in a hot oven for 50 minutes at 200 degrees Fahrenheit.
10. Remove from the molds and place in individual serving shells. Pour fresh cream around and grated gruyere cheese on top of the soufflés.
11. Place the soufflés back in a 350-degree Fahrenheit hot oven for 5 minutes.
- **Serve immediately.**

BRUCE OLIVER, TRAVEL ADVISOR & TV HOST

You deserve the best

SENSATIONAL CRUISE LINE CUISINES

Uniworld River Cruise Line – Black Forest Cake

Ingredients (Yield: 1 10-inch cake):

For Chocolate Sponge cake:
- 90 grams' all-purpose flour
- 50 grams' pastry flour
- 1 teaspoon baking soda
- 30 grams' coca powder (unsweetened)
- 6 eggs
- 170 grams' sugar
- 1/2 teaspoon salt

For cherry filling:
- 1 ounce (3 cl) cherry juice
- 20 grams' cornstarch
- 20 grams' sugar
- 2000 grams' fresh sour cherries, pitted
- cinnamon sticks

For the Cherry Cream:
- teaspoons (1 cl) Kirschwasser
- 15 grams powdered sugar
- 200 grams' heavy cream

For Assembly:
- Additional Kirschwasser for garnish"
- Additional Whipped Cream
- Dark chocolate shavings
- Fresh Sour Cherries, pitted

Preparation:

For Chocolate Sponge cake:
1. Grease a 10-inch spring form pan (or use nonstick spray). Preheat oven to 400 degrees F (200 degrees C).
2. Sift together flour, baking soda, and cocoa powder.

There are many versions of Black Forest Cake (also known as Schwarzwälder Kirschtorte). This recipe for Black Forest Cake is the one that was served on board the S.S. Antoinette. We like the subtle sweetness and pronounced flavor of the Kirschwasser in the cake. Once the cake is assembled, it is best refrigerated overnight and then garnished with more whipped cream, chocolate shavings, and fresh cherries and then served immediately.

Wine Recommendation: (Adirondack Winery, 2016), Merlot. This dry Merlot is medium-bodied, soft and silky, with fruit forward tones of dark berry, and a touch of brown spice and herbs that leaves a luscious texture on the palate. Enjoy it with beef, tomato-based dishes, dark fruit or chocolate desserts, and sharp or aged cheeses.

3. Combine eggs, sugar, and salt in a mixing bowl. Place the bowl over hot water bath and whisk constantly until the temperature reaches about 110 degrees F (44 degrees C).
4. Whisk on high speed until the mixture has cooled, is foamy, and has turned pale yellow.
5. Incorporate cocoa-flour mixture, being careful to deflate the foam as little as possible.
6. Incorporate the melted butter. Pour mixture into spring form pan. Bake at 400 degrees F (200 degrees C) until done, usually about 20 minutes.
7. Let cool on a wire rack and then careful remove from pan.

For Cherry Filling:
1. In a medium pan, melt the sugar without any caramelization. Add the juice, cherries, and cinnamon sticks and slowly bring to a boil.
2. Let simmer for a few minutes and then use the cornstarch for thickening. Once the mixture has thickened, remove from the heat and let cool.

For Cherry Cream:
1. Whip the cream until stiff peaks form.
2. Mix the Kirschwasser together with the powdered sugar and carefully fold into the whipped cream.

To Assemble Cake:
1. Cut the sponge cake into three layers and prepare 1st layer by soaking the sponge cake with Kirschwasser. Fill one layer with 1/3 cherry cream and then top with 1/3 cherry filling and cover with 2nd layer of sponge cake. Soak the 2nd layer again with Kirschwasser and repeat layer of 1/3 cherry cream and 1/3 cherry filling. Top with 3rd layer and again soak with Kirschwasser. Top with remaining cherry cream and cherry filling. Refrigerate overnight.
2. Garnish with addition whipped cream, chocolate shavings, and fresh sour cherries.

SENSATIONAL CRUISE LINE CUISINES

Chef Claudio and the Culinary Team on the S. S. Antoinette
Uniworld Boutique River Cruise Collection

0-18 *Photos courtesy of UniWorld*

SS Antoinette Chef

Buffet

Inaugural Cruise 2012

BRUCE OLIVER, TRAVEL ADVISOR & TV HOST

Viking River Cruise - Beef Stroganoff

Ingredients (makes 4-5 servings):
2 lbs. high-quality beef, prime cut (filet or sirloin)
Salt and pepper
5 Tbsp. flour, divided
1 medium onion, diced
8 oz. button mushrooms, cut in half (optional)
1 Tbsp. butter
4 Tbsp. demi-glace*
2 Cup beef broth
5 oz. sour cream

Preparation:
1. Slice meat along the grain into strips 1-inch long and 1/4-inch wide. Season meat with salt and pepper. Toss meat in four tablespoons of flour, reserving one tablespoon of flour for sauce. In a preheated pan, sauté meat until brown. Remove meat from pan and set aside. Add onions (and mushrooms if using) to pan and continue sautéing until a light brown.
2. Melt butter in a skillet and add remaining tablespoon of flour. Continue to cook on low heat for about 2 minutes, stirring continuously. Add demi-glace, beef broth and sour cream. Salt and pepper to taste. Stir all ingredients together thoroughly. Add meat, onions and mushrooms; heat very gently for 15 minutes, making sure not to let stew simmer or boil.

*You can buy demi-glace at a gourmet shop like Williams-Sonoma or Whole Foods, or in packets on amazon.com. If you do not have demi-glace, you can use a high-quality beef stock or consommé and cook it down to thicken and bring out the flavor.

> **Wine Recommendation**: (Marimar Estate Don Miguel Vineyard (Sebastopol, CA), 2016), Mas Cavalls Pinot Noir. There's a really rich pinot fruit to complement the beef and mushrooms, and a good acid backbone to work through the cream. Elegant nose, with classic varietal aromas of wild cherry, clove and sandlewood plus the characteristic note of forest floor from this special vineyard. The tannins are supple and graceful, and the palate is round, complex and fleshy. Alixe Lischett of Cabernet & Company in Glen Ellyn says: "I would recommend serving it at cellar temperature, between 58-60° F."

Serving Suggestion - Serve over buttered pasta, rice or potato straws.

SENSATIONAL CRUISE LINE CUISINES

Spice Usage Tips*

	Appetizers	Soups	Eggs & Cheese	Meats	Fish & Seafood	Salads	Sauces & Relishes	Vegetables	Breads & Desserts
Allspice	Meatballs	Split Pea Oyster Stew Bean		Ham Beef Stew Meat Loaf Jerk Chicken	Spiced Shrimp Poached Fish	Pickled Beets	Catsup Chili Sauce	Sweet Potatoes, Asparagus, Beets Broccoli, Cabbage, Peas, Carrots, Zucchini, Winter Squash	Cookies, Cakes, Pies Coffee Cakes, Pudding Baked Custard, Fruit Hot Spiced Beverages
Basil	Seafood Cocktail Tomato Juice Cheese Spreads	Minestrone Beef, Tomato Vegetable, Chicken	Cheese Soufflé Scrambled Eggs Omelets, Quiche Deviled Eggs	Beef Stew Roast & Fried Chicken Italian Foods Hamburgers, Roasts	Baked & Poached Fish Tuna & Salmon Loaf	Chicken Tuna Seafood Vegetable	Spaghetti Cheese Sauce Barbeque Sauce Marinara Sauce	Asparagus, Beets, Broccoli, Carrots, Corn, Peas, Cabbage, Green Beans, Potatoes, Tomatoes, Winter Squash, Zucchini	Herb Bread Breadsticks Focaccia
Bay		Bean Vegetable Beef Chicken		Stews Corned Beef Pot Roast	Poached Fish Spiced Shrimp, Boiled Shrimp	Aspic	Tomato Sauce Spaghetti Sauce Barbeque Sauce	Potatoes	
Caraway Seed	Cheese Spread	Borscht Potato	Cottage Cheese	Sauerbraten Stews		Coleslaw Pickled Beets		Cabbage, Carrots, Sauerkraut	Cookies Rye Bread

BRUCE OLIVER, TRAVEL ADVISOR & TV HOST

	Appetizers	Soups	Eggs & Cheese	Meats	Fish & Seafood	Salads	Sauces & Relishes	Vegetables	Breads & Desserts
Celery Seed	Meatballs, Dips Cheese Spreads Seafood Cocktail Tomato Juice	Vegetable Tomato	Cottage Cheese Deviled Eggs	Stews, Pot Roasts Meatloaf	Baked Fish	Shrimp, Tuna Potato Salad Dressing Coleslaw	Barbeque Sauce Cocktail Sauce	Potatoes, Cauliflower, Green Beans, Peas, Tomatoes	Biscuits Muffins
Chili Powder	Cheese Spreads Shrimp Cocktail Nachos Salsa	Chili, Beef, Bean, Vegetable Gazpacho	Omelets Deviled Eggs	Fajitas Stews, Hamburgers Roast & Fried Chicken Tacos	Baked Fish		Bean Taco	Taco Sauce Barbeque Sauce Tomato Sauce	Corn, Cauliflower, Green Beans, Peas, Tomatoes
Cinnamon	Fruit Cocktail	Split Pea Fruit	Cottage Cheese Dessert Omelet	Stews Braised Meats Chicken Stuffing Ham		Fruit	Chutney, Catsup Mole Sauce Fruit Sauce, Relishes Chocolate Sauce	Beets, Carrots, Corn, Winter Squash, Sweet Potatoes	Coffee Cakes, Pies, Fruit, Muffins, Yeast Breads, Cakes, Cookies, Puddings, Hot Spiced Beverages
Cloves	Fruit Cocktail Cranberry Juice Apple Cider	Split Pea	Eggnog Fruit Omelet	Ham, Braised Meats Corned Beef Roast Chicken	Poached Fish Spiced Shrimp	Pickled Beets	Chutney Relishes	Beets, Carrots, Cabbage, Winter Squash, Sweet Potato	Coffee Cake, Cake Cookies, Pies Pudding, Fruit Hot Spiced Beverages
Cumin	Nachos Meatballs Guacamole	Chili Vegetable Beef Gazpacho	Scrambled Eggs Omelets, Quiche	Roast Beef Pork Chicken Mexican Dishes	Fish Tacos	Avocado Marinated Vegetables Bean	Barbeque Sauce Mexican Sauce	Tomatoes, Green Beans Corn Zucchini	

SENSATIONAL CRUISE LINE CUISINES

								Vegetable Sauce	
Curry Powder	Shrimp & Seafood Cocktails Dips Spreads	Chicken Beef Seafood	Deviled Eggs Scrambled Eggs Egg Salad	Curries Chicken, Beef, Veal, Lamb, Roasts Stews	Shrimp Creamed Tuna or Salmon	Marinated Vegetable Chicken Seafood	Cream Sauce Chutney		Broccoli, Cabbage, Carrots, Cauliflower, Corn, Green Beans, Peas, Potatoes, Zucchini
Dill weed	Dips Spreads Fish & Seafood Cocktails	Chicken Split Pea Potato Chowders	Deviled, Scrambled & Creamed Eggs, Quiche, Soufflés, Omelets, Cottage Cheese	Lamb, Veal & Pork Roasts Chicken Casseroles Hamburgers	Tuna or Salmon Loaf Seafood Casseroles Baked & Broiled Fish	Chicken, Shrimp, Vegetable Potato, Cucumber Coleslaw	Cheese Sauce Cream Sauce Relishes		Asparagus, Beets, Green Beans, Broccoli, Cabbage, Potatoes, Carrots, Cauliflower, Corn, Peas, Tomatoes, Zucchini

* NOTE: This table is being used with compliments of ACH Foods, Inc.

	Appetizers	Soups	Eggs & Cheese	Meats	Fish & Seafood	Salads	Sauces & Relishes	Vegetables	Breads & Desserts
Garlic	Dips Spreads	Chicken Vegetable	Omelets	Roast Chicken Burgers Italian, Mexican or Asian Dishes	Baked Fish Shrimp Scampi	Vegetable Potato Salad Dressings	Italian-Style Sauces Barbeque Sauce	Mashed or Roasted Potatoes, Tomatoes, Zucchini	Breadsticks Focaccia French Bread
Ginger	Broiled Grapefruit	Split Pea Bean Fruit		Marinades Ham, Braised Meats Stir-Fry	Marinades	Fruit Chicken	Chutney Relishes Fruit	Asparagus, Beets, Carrots, Winter Squash, Sweet Potatoes, Stir-fried Vegetables	Coffee Cakes Gingerbread Cake, Fruit Cookies
Marjoram	Dips Spreads	Vegetable, Beef Chicken, Onion, Seafood, Fish Tomato	Scrambled Eggs Quiche, Soufflé Omelet	Stews, Roast & Fried Chicken, Meat Loaf Meat Balls, Roasts	Baked & Broiled Fish	Marinated Vegetable Chicken	Italian Sauce Tomato Sauce Cream Sauce	Asparagus, Broccoli, Cabbage, Carrots, Cauliflower, Corn, Green Beans, Peas, Potatoes, Tomatoes, Squash	
Mustard	Dips Meat Spreads Meatballs Pretzels	Chili	Omelets Quiche Deviled Eggs Egg Salad	Sausage Pork Ham Chicken	Baked & Broiled Fish	Vegetable Potato Coleslaw Salad Dressings	Honey Mustard Barbeque Marinades	Baked Beans Marinated Vegetables Pickles	
Nutmeg	Fruit Cocktail	Split Pea Chowders	Quiche Fruit Omelet Eggnog	Veal, Ham Meat Loaf Sausage		Chicken Fruit	Cream Sauce Dessert Sauces Chocolate Sauce	Asparagus, Beets, Broccoli, Cabbage, Potatoes, Carrots, Cauliflower, Green Beans, Peas, Squash, Sweet Potatoes	Muffins, Custard, Coffee Cakes, Cookies Pudding, Fruit, Pies

SENSATIONAL CRUISE LINE CUISINES

	Appetizers	Soups	Eggs & Cheese	Meats	Fish & Seafood	Salads	Sauces & Relishes	Vegetables	Breads & Desserts
Oregano	Dips Spreads Meatballs Tomato Juice	Minestrone Tomato, Beef Vegetable, Bean	Soufflés, Quiche Omelets, Scrambled & Deviled Eggs	Roast & Fried Chicken Meat Loaf Roasts, Stews Braised Meats	Baked & Broiled Fish Shrimp	Bean Vegetable Potato Salad Dressings	Italian-Style Sauce Spaghetti Sauce Tomato Sauce Barbeque Sauce	Asparagus, Broccoli, Corn, Green Beans, Peas, Roasted Potatoes, Tomatoes, Zucchini	Muffins Biscuits Herb Breads
Rosemary	Meatballs	Chicken Pea	Soufflés Scrambled Eggs	Roast Lamb Veal Chicken Pork Roasts	Broiled & Poached Fish	Tomatoes Salad Dressings Cucumber	Gravy	Corn, Green Beans, Peas, Roasted Potatoes, Tomatoes, Zucchini	
Sage	Cheese Spreads Meatballs	Chicken Pea Tomato	Soufflés Quiche, Omelets Creamed & Scrambled Eggs	Chicken & Pork Dishes Stuffing Sausage	Stuffed Fish Baked Fish Broiled Fish	Salad Dressings	Poultry Gravy	Green Beans, Brussels Sprouts, Peas, Zucchini	Muffins Biscuits
Tarragon	Cheese Spreads Seafood Cocktail Pate Tomato Juice	Chicken Vegetable Tomato	Omelets, Soufflés, Quiche Deviled & Creamed Eggs	Chicken & Pork Dishes Roast Pork, Veal, Lamb & Chicken	Broiled & Poached Fish Seafood	Tomatoes Cucumber Vegetable Salad Dressings	Hollandaise Poultry Gravy Béarnaise	Broccoli, Carrots, Cauliflower, Green Beans, Peas, Potatoes, Tomatoes, Zucchini	
Thyme	Cheese Spreads Dips Pate Seafood Cocktails	Vegetable, Pea Beef, Chicken Tomato, Bean Minestrone	Soufflés, Omelets Scrambled Eggs Cottage Cheese Quiche	Baked & Fried Chicken Braised Meats, Roasts, Pork Chops Stuffing	Baked & Broiled Fish Seafood	Salad Dressings Potato & Vegetable Salads, Tomatoes, Cucumbers	Hollandaise Gravy Tomato Sauce	Asparagus, Broccoli, Carrots, Cauliflower, Corn, Green Beans, Peas, Potatoes, Tomatoes, Zucchini, Brussels Sprouts, Onions	Herb Bread

* NOTE: This table is being used with the compliments of ACH Foods, Inc.

Spices used for Ethnic Foods

Column numbers corresponding with table below:

1 – Asian (a) (In addition stock: Soy sauce and/or Tamari, Rice Vinegar, Fish Sauce, Chili Sauce, Oyster Sauce, Coconut Milk, Miso Paste, Rice Wine, and Lime)

2 – Eastern European (e)   3 – French (f)

4 – Italian (i)   5 – Mediterranean (m)

6 – Mexican (x)   7 – Moroccan (x) (+ Almonds, Olive Oil)

8 – Spanish (s)   9 – Baking (b)

10 – Holiday Cooking & Baking (h)

SENSATIONAL CRUISE LINE CUISINES

	1	2	3	4	5	6	7	8	9	10
Allspice					m				b	h
Anise					m		x		b	
Annatto					m					
Apple Mint										
Basil				i	m					
Bay Leaves			f	i	m		x	s		
Bergamot										
Borage										
Caledula										
Caraway					m					
Cayenne Pepper							x			
Chamomile										
Cardamon			f		m				b	
Chervil					m					
Chili Pepper				i	m	x		s		
Chive			f		m					
Cilantro	a				m		x			
Cinnamon					m		x	m	b	h
Cloves					m		x		b	h
Coriander					m	x				
Cumin					m	x	x	m		
Curry	a									
Dill										
Fennel			f	i	m		x			
Fenugreek					m		x			
French Sorrel										
Garlic			f		m	x		s		
Ginger	a				m		x		b	

	1	2	3	4	5	6	7	8	9	10
Horehound										
Horseradish										
Hyssop										
Juniper Berry	e				m					
Lavender 👃										
Lemon Balm										
Lemon Verbena							x			
Lovage										
Mace	e				m		x		b	
Marjoram	e	f			m					
Mint	e				m		x			
Mustard	e									
Nutmeg	e	f			m		x		b	
Onion		f			m		x			
Oregano				i	m	x	x	s		
Orris Root										
Paprika	e				m		x			h
Parsley	e	f			m		x	s		
Pepper	e	f			m		x		b	
Poppy Seeds	e								b	
Red Pepper	a						x			
Rosemary		f	i		m			s		
Saffron		f			m		x	s		
Sage		f	i		m		x			h
Salad Burnet										
Savory					m					h
Sesame Seed	a						x		b	
Sweet Woodruff										
Tarragon		f			m					
Thyme		f	i		m		x			
Turmeric					m		x			
Vanilla 👃									b	

If you would like more information on Spices, Herbs & Salts then you should pick up my book "Secrets of Cooking (Scratch & Sniff) – Using Spices Herbs & Salts". Order Here: http://SensationalBookNews.com.

SENSATIONAL CRUISE LINE CUISINES

Herbs & Spices Around the World

The Difference Herbs vs. Spices

NOTE: Most the spices that we use today are from the Eastern Hemisphere and tropical destinations like South East Asia, India and the Mediterranean.

Did you know that a different part of the same plant can be used as an herb or a spice?
- Leafy green parts are usually used as an herb.
- Spices are usually seeds, flowers, root stems or the bark.

Bibliography

(n.d.). Retrieved from http://www.spiceadvice.com/newsa/usage/chart.html

10 Incredible Facts Sense of Smell. (2014). Retrieved from Everyday Health: http://www.everydayhealth.com/news/incredible-facts-about-your-sense-smell/

(1888). In J. Corson, *Cooking school text book and House Keepers Guide* (pp. 13-16). New York City: Orange Judd Company.

(1908). In *Condiments--Ginger, Whole and Ground--Specification*.

20 Facts Sense Smell. (2016). Retrieved from UK Mirror Lifestyle Magazine: http://www.mirror.co.uk/lifestyle/health/20-fascinating-facts-sense-smell-1977351

(2016). Retrieved from Sharpe Hill Vineyard, Pomfret, CT: http://sharpehill.com

(2016). Retrieved from Chateau Souverain, Sonoma County (California): http://www.souverain.com

ACH FOOD COMPANIES, I. -C. (2016). *Spice Advice - Spice Usage Tips*. Retrieved from http://www.spiceadvice.com/newsa/usage/chart.html

Adastra Winery. (2016). Retrieved from http://www.adastrawines.com/

Adirondack Winery. (2016). Retrieved from http://www.adirondackwinery.com

All Spice. (n.d.). Retrieved from http://Allspice.com

Artezin Wines. (2016). Retrieved from http://www.artezinwines.com/

Bailyn, L. (2006). *Breaking the Mold: Redesigning Work for Productive and Satisfying Lives.* Ithaca: ILr Press - Cornell University Press.

Baiting Hollow Farm Vinyard (Calverton, NY). (n.d.). Retrieved from http://www.baitinghollowfarmvineyard.com

Beringer. (2016). Retrieved from http://www.beringer.com/knights-valley

Billsboro Winery (Geneva, NY). (2016). Retrieved from www.billsborowinery.com

Brotherhood Winery (Washingtonville, NY). (2016). Retrieved from http://www.brotherhood-winery.com

Brotherhood Winery, (Washingtonville, NY). (2016). Retrieved from http://www.brotherhood-winery.com

Chateau Ste Michelle (Woodinville, WA). (2016). Retrieved from https://www.ste-michelle.com

Clinton Vineyards. (2016). Retrieved from http://www.clintonvineyards.com

Colored Eggs. (2016). Retrieved from http://www.hobbyfarms.com/7-chickens-to-raise-for-colorful-eggs-3/

Cruise with Bruce Show - Ryan talks travel. (2011). Retrieved from http://www.blogtalkradio.com/cruisewithbruce/2011/06/22/ryan-oreilly-heir-to-the-oreilly-auto-parts-talks-travel

Cruise with Bruce Show interview Boston Harbor Cruise. (2011). Retrieved from http://www.blogtalkradio.com/cruisewithbruce/2011/08/09/rags-to-riches-story-richard-oleary-spirit-of-boston-cruise

Cruise with Bruce Show with Rick Robinson's interview on Ireland and his book Manifest Destiny. (2011). Retrieved from http://www.blogtalkradio.com/cruisewithbruce/2011/03/30/rick-robinson-ireland-on-cruise-with-bruce-rick-robinson-talks-ireland-n-manifest-destiny

Cruise with Bruce YouTube Channel. (2014). Retrieved from https://www.youtube.com/watch?v=lqQnqKxIgbQ

Cullari Vineyards and Winery (Hershey, PA),. (2016). Retrieved from http://www.cullarivineyards.com

Der Pollerhof (Weinviertel, Austria). (2016). Retrieved from http://www.pollerhof.at/english-/index.html

Domaine Pierre Luneau-Papin. (2016). Retrieved from http://www.domaineluneaupapin.com

Dr. Frank's Vinifera Wine Cellars. (2016). Retrieved from http://www.drfrankwines.com

Dr. Michael Orzolek, P. o. (2016, N/A N/A). *Herb Directory.* (Penn State University) Retrieved from Penn State » Extension » Plants and Pests » Home Lawn and Garden » Herbs: http://extension.psu.edu/plants/gardening/herbs

Ellen Galinski, P. (2014, February 1). *Overwork in America: When the Way We Work Becomes Too Much.* Retrieved from Families and Work Institute: http://www.familiesandwork.org/overwork-in-america-when-the-way-we-work-becomes-too-much/

Fontana Candida Vineyards, Lazio, Italy. (2016).

Foodterms. (2016). Retrieved from http://www.foodterms.com/encyclopedia/celery-root/index.html?oc=linkback

Gibbs, W. M. (1854-1909). Spices. In W. M. Gibbs, *Spices and how to know them* (pp. 7-178). Buffalo, N.Y.: The Matthews-Northrup Works.

Girard Napa Valley. (2016). Retrieved from http://www.girardwinery.com

Goddard, F. B. (1888). Spices and Herbs. In F. B. Goddard, *Grocers' Goods: A Family Guide to the Purchase of Flour, Sugar, Tea, Coffee, Spices, Canned Goods, Cigars, Wines, and All Other Articles Usually Found in American Grocery Stores* (pp. 16,39-42,47). New York City: The Tradesmen's Publishing Company.

Green, M. E. (1894). In M. E. Green, *Condiments, spices and flavors.* Chicago: The Library of Congress.

Gump, B. B., & Matthews, K. A. (2000). In B. B. Gump, & K. A. Matthews, *Are Vacations Good for Your Health? The 9-Year Mortality Experience After the Multiple Risk Factor Intervention Trial* (pp. September/October 2000 - Volume 62 - Issue 5 - pp 608-612). American Psychosomatic Society.

Hayne Vineyard. (2016). Retrieved from http://www.chasecellars.com/hayne-vineyard/

Henry of Pelham Estate Winery, ON Canada. (2016). Retrieved from http://henryofpelham.com/

Hertzler, A. A. (Reprinted 2001). Herbs and Spices. *Publication 348-907.*

Holland America Line Interview. (2011). Retrieved from http://www.blogtalkradio.com/cruisewithbruce/2011/05/04/holland-america-line-cruise-with-bruce-radios-cruise-news

Jazz musician Chris Geith Cruise with Bruce as we talk about his boyhood home and favorite vacations to Lake Como. (2011). Retrieved from http://www.blogtalkradio.com/cruisewithbruce/2011/02/23/chris-geith-music-on-cruise-with-bruce-chris-geith-talks-milan-italy-weather-channel-jazz-music

Jonathan Edwards Winery. (2016). Retrieved from www.jedwardswinery.com

Jonathan Edwards Winery, Stonington, CT. (2016). Retrieved from www.jedwardswinery.com

LaBelle Winery (Amherst, NH) . (2016). Retrieved from http://www.labellewinerynh.com

Marenco Vini Winery. (2016). Retrieved from Marenco Vini Winery: http://en.marencovini.com/

Marimar Estate Don Miguel Vineyard (Sebastopol, CA). (2016). Retrieved from http://marimarestate.com/don-miguel-vineyard

Marques de Caceres. (2016). Retrieved from http://www.marquesdecaceres.com/?lang=en

Mary E. Green, M. (1894). *Condiments, Spices and Flavors.* Library of Congress.

Masciarelli Winery. (2016).

Medicinal Plants. (2015, 11 23). Retrieved from Library of Congress - Science Reference Services: https://www.loc.gov/rr/scitech/tracer-bullets/medicplantstb.html

Michele Chiarlo Nivole. (2016).

Middle Ridge Winery. (2016). Retrieved from http://www.middleridge.com

Mitchum, L. (2014, 12 8). Press Officer. *The London Eye AKA EDF Energy London Eye & The Millennium Wheel | Bruce Oliver.* (B. Oliver, Interviewer) Cruise with Bruce Radio Show. Retrieved from http://www.blogtalkradio.com/cruisewithbruce/2014/12

/08/the-london-eye-aka-edf-energy-london-eye-the-millennium-wheel-bruce-oliver-1

Mount Palomar. (2016). Retrieved from
    http://www.mountpalomarwinery.com

Mount Palomar Vineyard. (2016). Retrieved from
    http://www.mountpalomarwinery.com

Mount Palomar Winery. (2016). Retrieved from
    http://www.mountpalomarwinery.com

NASA Earth Observatory. (2014). Retrieved from
    http://earthobservatory.nasa.gov/IOTD/view.php?id=85900

Ordering Wine. (2014). Retrieved from
    http://www.businessinsider.com/what-not-to-do-when-ordering-wine-2013-12

Otter Cove and Oh Wines - Monteray, CA. (2016). Retrieved from www.ottercovewines.com

Paradise Hills Winery (Wallingford, CT). (2016). Retrieved from http://paradisehillsvineyard.com/wine-menu/

Paradise Hills Winery (Wallingford, CT). (2016). Retrieved from http://paradisehillsvineyard.com/wine-menu/

Paradise Hills Winery, Wallingford, CT. (2016). Retrieved from http://paradisehillsvineyard.com/

Pellegrini Vineyards, Cutchogue, NY. (2016). Retrieved from http://pellegrinivineyards.com

Photo by FotoosVanRobin; cc. (n.d.).

Premier Cru Vineyard. (n.d.). Retrieved from
    http://www.billaud-simon.com/en/

Premier Cru Vineyard. (2016). Retrieved from
    http://www.billaud-simon.com/en/

Radio Show. (2014). Retrieved from
    http://www.blogtalkradio.com/cruisewithbruce/2014/12/12/history-of-cliveden-house--waldorf-astor-estate-taplow-birkshire-uk-england

Rainbow Eggs. (2016). Retrieved from
    http://www.fresheggsdaily.com/2012/02/rainbow-of-egg-colors.html

Robert Mondavi Winery. (2016). Retrieved from
    http://www.robertmondaviwinery.com

Saffron. (2016). Retrieved from
http://espacepourlavie.ca/en/saffron
Saracco Winery's. (2016). Retrieved from
http://www.paolosaracco.it/en/
Sense of Smell. (2013). Retrieved from
http://www.ncbi.nlm.nih.gov/pubmedhealth/PMHT0025081/
Sense of Taste. (2012). Retrieved from
http://www.ncbi.nlm.nih.gov/pubmedhealth/PMH0072592/
Sharpe Hill Vineyard (Pomfret, CT). (2016). Retrieved from
http://sharpehill.com
Simon, B. (2016). Retrieved from http://www.thekitchn.com
Summers Winery, Calistoga, CA. (2016). Retrieved from
https://www.summerswinery.com
Taylor Brooke Winery. (2016). Retrieved from
http://taylorbrookwinery.com
Willamette Valley Vineyards. (2016). Retrieved from
http://wvv.com
Windsor Vineyards (Healdsburg, CA). (2016). Retrieved from
http://www.windsorvineyards.com

BRUCE OLIVER, TRAVEL ADVISOR & TV HOST

Interactive Resources

Website: http://www.BruceLuxuryTravel.com
Blog : http://LuxuryTravelAdviserPodcast.com
Quarterly Sweepstakes: http://Win.CruiseWithBruce.com
Contact: http://VirtualLuxury.net/contact
Facebook: http://www.facebook.com/cruiseradionetwork
http://www.facebook.com/cruisewithbruce
http://www.facebook.com/groups/BruceOliverTV
Twitter: http://www.twitter.com/BruceOliverCT
YouTube: http://www.youtube.com/cruisewithbruce
Blog Talk Radio:
http://www.blogtalkradio.com/cruisewithbruce/podcast
iTunes: https://itunes.apple.com/us/podcast/food-wine-art-theme-based/id400027948?mt=2
TuneIn Radio:
http://tunein.com/radio/Cruise-with-Bruce-p382915/
Instagram: https://instagram.com/bruceoliverct/
Pinterest: https://www.pinterest.com/cruisewithbruce/
Scratch and Sniff Travel™
http://ScratchAndSniffTravel.com
Bruce Oliver, Scent-sational Traveler™
http://scentsationaltraveler.com/
Scent-Sational Travel™ Books
http://ScentsationalTravelBooks.com
Promotions http://Promotions.CruiseWithBruce.com
Yelp https://www.yelp.com/biz/virtual-luxury-network-cruise-with-bruce-enterprises-greenwich
Bruce Oliver TV: http://BruceOliverTV
Smart TV Network: http://SmartTVtraveler.com
Travel Coloring Books: http://TravelingColoringBooks.com

Index

Allspice.................70
Antarctica...........33
Apple Pie..............24
Basil......................70
BBQ Sauce............51
Beef......................68
Black Forest Cake 64
BRUCE OLIVER
  Bruce................85
Budapest..............15
Cake......................64
Caraway Seed...........70
Celery Seed............71
Cheese...................62
  Cheese Soufflé .62
  Farmer's Cheese
  Fritters..............18
Chili Powder...........71
Cinnamon...............71
Cloves....................71
Crab......................22
Cumin....................71
Curry Powder...........72
Dessert
  Apple Pie.........24
  Cake..................64
Dillweed.................72
Duck.....................47
Falkland Islands 33
Fettuccine.............53
Fritters.................18
Garlic....................73
Ginger....................73
Hungarian Goulash15, 16

Hungry
  Budapest..........15
Lousiana
  New Orleans....22
Marinades and
Sauces
  BBQ Sauce.......51
Marjoram.................73
Mustard..................73
Nashville...............24
Nutmeg..................73
Oregano..................74
Pasta
  Fettuccine Alfredo 53
  Ravioli Filled with
  Ricotta..............31
Pie
  American Queen
  Apple Pie.........24
Ravioli...................31
Rib Eye................43
Rosemary...............74
Sage......................74
Scallops..........37, 59
Seafood
  Jumbo Lump Crab 22
  Pan Seared Scallops
 59
  Pan Seared Scallops
  with Red Curry Glaze
 59
  Seared Scallops 37
  Warm Lobster..29
Soufflé.................62
Syunik.................18

Tarragon 74
Tennesse
  Nashville 24
Thyme 74

United States
  Mississippi River 22, 24
  Warm Lobster 29

SENSATIONAL CRUISE LINE CUISINES

Win Sweepstakes

Scan the QR Code above to enter Signature Travel Network's Quarterly Sweepstakes.
http://Win.CruiseWithBruce.com

Every quarter we award an all-inclusive vacation to one lucky winner.

BRUCE OLIVER, TRAVEL ADVISOR & TV HOST

Scan the QR Code above to get a quarterly subscription to a 68-page Travel Magazine
http://Win.CruiseWithBruce.com

Enter all of the information that is requested and be sure to click on email notifications.

About Bruce Oliver – This book is an introduction to the Sensational Travel & Food Series and the Traveling Coloring Books.

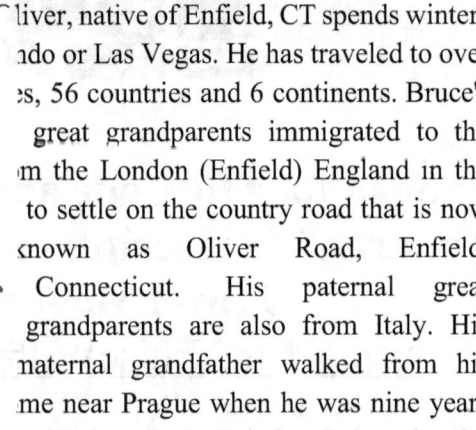

Bruce Oliver, native of Enfield, CT spends winters in Colorado or Las Vegas. He has traveled to over 90 cruises, 56 countries and 6 continents. Bruce's maternal great grandparents immigrated to the USA from the London (Enfield) England in the 1700's to settle on the country road that is now well known as Oliver Road, Enfield, Connecticut. His paternal great grandparents are also from Italy. His maternal grandfather walked from his home near Prague when he was nine years old to take a boat to America from Great Britain. Quite a feat for a nine-year old.

Bruce has a passion for global travel and photography.

He's the recipient of the Travel Weekly Silver Magellan Award for individuals in the travel industry and was awarded the 2014 Best of Enfield Cruise Agents. He's an affiliate of Palm Coast Travel and the Signature Travel Network.

Bruce has certification with the Cruise Line Industry Association (CLIA) and has credentials from the International Air Transport Association (IATA). He is a Luxury Travel Specialist and has "destination specialist" certifications from all over the world as well as a close working relationship with most the cruise lines and travel operators. He is a Level 2 Member of the United Nations Educational, Scientific, and Cultural Organization (AKA - UNESCO): World Heritage Convention.

He also has **travel photographer** press credentials from the

National Press Association and the **ITWPA**. He is a Professional Photographer registered with the International VR Photography Association (IVRPA) specializing in 360° Virtual Tours. He's listed as a **Charter Member of the Library of Congress** and the **Microsoft Alumni Association**.

He's the recipient of many honors and awards in his community and higher education. In 1989, he graduated with a MBA from the University of Hartford. Bruce is listed in **MARQUIS: Who's Who in America, Who's Who in the World** and **Who's Who in American Education**. In 2019, Bruce was recognized by **Albert Nelson Marquis with the Lifetime Achievement Award** after being listed as a biographical reference in 68 diverse publications. Bruce has been a member of the National Eagle Scouts Association since 1967 and is a Vigil Honor Member in BSA's: Order of the Arrow. While attending high school, he was awarded the DeKalb Agricultural Accomplishment Award and the Connecticut State Farmer Degree from the Future Farmers of America.

For more books on travel please visit:
http://SensationalTravelBooks.com

*Please write a **Review on Amazon** for this book. I am always interested in getting feedback and would love to hear what you would like me to include in the next edition. Thanks, Bruce*

http://Amazon.com/author/bruceoliver

http://BarnesAndNoble.com

---

[i] Amawaterways River Cruises: http://travelurl.net/Amawaterways-Budapest
[ii] American Cruise Line: http://travelurl.net/AmCruiseLines
[iii] American Cruise Line: http://travelurl.net/AmericanQueen
[iv] Crystal Cruises: http://travelurl.net/CrystalCruiseLine
[v] Cunard Cruise Line: http://travelurl.net/CunardCruiseLine
[vi] Holland America Line: http://travelurl.net/HollandAmericaCruises
[vii] Oceania Cruise Line: http://travelurl.net/OceaniaCruise
[viii] Paul Gauguin Cruises: http://travelurl.net/PaulGauguinCruises
[ix] Princess Cruise Line: http://travelurl.net/princess-cruises
[x] Regent Seven Seas: http://travelurl.net/RegentSevenSeasCruises
[xi] Seabourn: http://travelurl.net/Seabourn-Cruise

www.ingramcontent.com/pod-product-compliance
Lightning Source LLC
LaVergne TN
LVHW020937090426
835512LV00020B/3401